Dr. Jonathan Rashied Wilson Jr.

Catto and Caroline:

Riding for Freedom

Written By: Jonathan Rashied Wilson Jr.

LIBRARY OF CONGRESS CATALOGING IN PUBLICATION DATA
First Edition:
Print Version ISBN: 979-8-9926327-2-9

Copyright © 2025 by Dr. Jonathan Rashied Wilson Jr.

All rights reserved. No part of this book may be reproduced or transmitted in any form or by any means, electronic or mechanical, including photocopying, recording, or by any information storage and retrieval system, without permission in writing from the author, except for the inclusion of brief quotations in a review.

DEDICATION

For all the brave young hearts who dare to dream of a fairer world. May you always ride for freedom.

ABOUT THE AUTHOR

Dr. Jonathan Rashied Wilson Jr. is and author, educator, and civil rights advocate whose work reflect his unwavering passion for African American history and social justice, he has dedicated his career to uncovering and sharing the powerful, often overlooked stories of those who fought for equality during America's most challenging times.

His engaging storytelling and meticulous research have brought historical events—such as the courageous struggle to desegregate Philadelphia's streetcars—to life for readers of all ages. Through his work, he illuminates the triumphs and trials of civil rights pioneers, inspiring young minds to appreciate the importance of activism and community unity.

Known for his interdisciplinary approach, Dr. Wilson skillfully combines narrative history with innovative educational techniques. He is committed to making history accessible and relevant, mentoring students and actively participating in community outreach. His dedication to public history has earned him recognition from numerous historical societies and educational institutions.

Dr. Wilson's legacy is one of courage, resilience, and the enduring belief that every young person can contribute to a more just and equitable future. When he isn't researching or writing, he continues to work tirelessly to ensure that the lessons of the past guide the leaders of tomorrow.

Catto and Caroline

The streets of the 7th Ward bustled with the energy of a new day. Merchants opened their shops. The scent of fresh bread and morning coal filled the air. In the heart of Philadelphia's Black community, hope lived on every corner. A central hub of Black life, activism, and culture during Reconstruction.

Octavius Catto, a respected teacher and activist, often walked with his girlfriend Caroline confidently past brick homes and gas lamps of Reconstruction-era Philadelphia, nodding to neighbors who admired their love. They met as Students at the Institute for Colored Youth on 8th and Bainbridge. As two of the school's brightest scholars and now activists, they had a bold vision of a city where Black people rode streetcars freely, taught in every school, and voted without fear.

Caroline called out, "Octavius! Ready for the meeting?" he smiled. "Born ready. Let's change the city, one step at a time."

In 1867, the laws of the city said nothing about segregation on public streetcars. That silence allowed racism to speak loudly. Streetcar conductors refused to pick up Black passengers. Caroline had once been left standing in the rain as an empty car rolled by. She remembered the humiliation—and the anger.

Octavius knew that the streetcars represented more than transportation. They represented access: to jobs, to schools, to freedom itself. If they were denied that ride, they were denied progress. "If our people can fight for the Union," he would often say, "then we deserve the right to ride."

They began recording incidents of refusal. Each entry was a blow against injustice.

Since a student at the prestigious Institute for Colored Youth, Caroline had always believed in the power of education. As one of the first Black women to pass the city's teacher's exam, she taught with passion and purpose. Each lesson was a chance to uplift the next generation.

But even as a respected teacher, she was denied equal seating on public streetcars. "What lesson does that teach our children?" she asked her students one morning. "That injustice is normal? Never. We will change this. Together."

The children listened with wide eyes. One boy raised his hand. "Miss LeCount, will we ride one day too?"

"Yes," she said firmly. "Not just ride. We'll own the road."

Caroline stepped onto the streetcar. Her heart pounded, but her eyes were steady.

"You can't ride," the conductor snapped.

"I am a citizen of Philadelphia," she replied. "And I have paid my fare."

He refused to move. But Caroline didn't step back. The passengers stared, caught between curiosity and contempt. When she was finally forced off, she wrote everything down: time, location, words. It would be used in court. The first ride was denied, but the war for justice was gaining steam.

That evening, at the Equal Rights League, Caroline and Octavius outlined their plan. First, survey the routes on a map, and collect testimonies. Then, challenge conductors. Finally, push the state legislature to pass a law.

They recruited witnesses, including veterans, mothers, and ministers. Every story added weight to their cause. They wanted peace, but they would not be passive. "We must be brave," Octavius declared. "Even if they push us off the cars, we will return." Caroline nodded. "They may shut doors, but we'll open minds."

Caroline poured her experiences into a journal—her testimony, her resistance. The journal became her companion and her record of truth. Each entry was a lantern in a dark tunnel, illuminating the path ahead. She wrote of courage and cruelty. Of children who dreamed and men who threatened, of conductors who shoved her and riders who pretended not to see. Her experiences would later guide historians and inspire students.

The protests were silent but powerful. Groups of Black Philadelphians stood at car stops, refusing to leave until they were allowed to board. Their unity was their weapon, and their dignity fueled their resistance.

Octavius led with calm strength. He reminded everyone, "We are not asking for a ride. We are demanding recognition of our dignity as a people."

When some conductors closed the doors and sped away, the protestors stood taller.

One of the most impactful moments came when pregnant women joined the protest. Their bravery silenced even the most hardened conductors. No one could deny their right to ride.

Mrs. Hannah Banks, a widow carrying her second child, stepped aboard with her fare ready. The conductor looked away. He knew.

Caroline watched, heart swelling. "They can't ignore us all," she whispered.

"We are not asking for special treatment," Octavius said. "We are demanding equal rights. The right to travel, to learn. To live."

His words rang across the cobblestone streets. Newspapers published his speech. Ministers repeated it from pulpits. Young men memorized it.

Caroline wrote in her journal, "Today, the city heard us. Tomorrow, they must obey."

In March of 1867, the Pennsylvania legislature passed a bill prohibiting segregation on streetcars. It was a historic moment. It didn't end racism, but it ended a symbol of it.

Octavius stood in silent celebration. The law was theirs, but it belonged to every voice that had spoken up.

For the first time, Catto and Caroline boarded a streetcar and weren't stopped. She took her seat. No one whispered. No one blocked her. She rode through the city like she belonged—because she did. The ride lasted only minutes, but it echoed through time.

Although the Pennsylvania legislature had passed the law banning streetcar segregation, some conductors still refused to comply. One afternoon, Caroline boarded a car and was told she could not ride.

She didn't argue. Instead, she stepped out of the car, went to the mayor's office, and requested a printed copy of the law. With the official document in hand, she returned to the same line and presented it to the conductor. He stepped aside.

On Election Day, October 10, 1871, as he helped Black voters reach the polls, Octavius Catto was shot and killed by an Irish white supremacist. His death shocked the city.

Caroline wept, but she didn't stop. She taught harder. She marched longer. She kept the journal alive.

Caroline promised to continue the work. As a teacher, she taught not only reading and math but also history. She told the truth about Catto, her first love, and the price of his courage. Her students would carry the fire well into the 20th century.

Octavius Valentine Catto (1839–1871) was an educator, writer, orator, tutor to Fredrick Douglass, and civil rights activist. He taught at the Institute for Colored Youth in Philadelphia, now Cheyney University, where he inspired generations of Black teachers. He fought for the rights of African Americans to ride streetcars, vote in elections, and serve in the military during the Civil War. On October 10, 1871, Catto was shot and killed in Philadelphia while helping Black men vote. He was only 32 years old. Today, he is honored with a statue at Philadelphia's City Hall—the first monument there to an individual African American.

Caroline LeCount (1846–1923) was a trailblazing educator and activist. She became one of the first Black women to pass the city's teacher examination and was appointed to teach in Philadelphia's public schools. As Catto's partner in life and activism, LeCount played a critical role in desegregating the city's streetcars. She continued to teach and fight for justice long after his death, preserving his legacy and raising generations of children to believe in freedom and fairness.

Together, Octavius and Caroline helped transform Philadelphia—and inspired movements that would follow for over a century.

- 1839 – Octavius Catto is born in Charleston, South Carolina.
- 1846 – Caroline LeCount is born in Philadelphia, Pennsylvania.
- 1854 – Institute for Colored Youth relocates to Philadelphia; Catto becomes a student, later a teacher.
- 1863 – Catto helps recruit Black soldiers for the Union Army during the Civil War.
- 1865 – Civil War ends; slavery is abolished with the 13th Amendment.
- 1866–1867 – Octavius and Caroline lead desegregation protests against streetcars in Philadelphia.
- March 1867 – Pennsylvania legislature passes a law banning segregation on streetcars.
- 1871 – Catto is murdered while assisting Black voters on Election Day.
- 1923 – Caroline LeCount dies, having served nearly 50 years as a teacher.
- 2017 – A statue of Octavius Catto is unveiled at Philadelphia City Hall.

This book is a work of historical fiction based entirely on real people, real events, and documented sources. The words spoken by Octavius Catto in this story are inspired by his public speeches and writings, preserved in historical archives. Caroline LeCount's strength and bravery are evident in newspaper accounts, teacher records, and the journals she reportedly kept.

Study Guide Questions

1. Why were streetcars such a powerful symbol for Octavius and Caroline?
2. How did Caroline LeCount use the law to challenge injustice?
3. What role did peaceful protest play in the story?
4. Why was education important to Caroline?
5. How do the actions of Octavius and Caroline continue to impact us today?

Glossary
- Segregation: The enforced separation of different racial groups.
- Streetcar: A public vehicle on tracks used for city transportation.
- Protest: A public demonstration against injustice.
- Desegregation: The process of ending separation based on race.
- Legislation: A law or set of laws made by a government.

About the Author
Dr. Jonathan Rashied Wilson Jr.
Founder of the Fathership Foundation and author committed to telling powerful, pride-filled Black history for children. He believes truth can inspire the next generation of leaders.

Additional Reading and Sources
- Biddle, Daniel R., and Murray Dubin. Tasting Freedom: Octavius Catto and the Battle for Equality
- Foner, Eric. Reconstruction: America's Unfinished Revolution
- Giesberg, Judith. Emilie Davis's Civil War
- Temple University Blockson Collection
- Historical Society of Pennsylvania
- Smith, Jessie Carney. Black Firsts

www.ingramcontent.com/pod-product-compliance
Lightning Source LLC
Chambersburg PA
CBHW040907020526
44114CB00038B/88